THE BOAT RACE

"Heave-ho!" called Patchy Fog, as Miss T. helped him haul their old yacht, *Morning Cloud,* out of the Weatherly Hills boathouse.

It was the morning of the big boat race, which was a very special event in Weatherly Hills, with everybody who had a boat taking part.

Patchy and Miss T. were the first ones on the beach. "The old craft looks a bit worse for the wear," said Miss T.

"Just look at the state this sail's in," Miss T. went on. "It's all patched up and full of dust. We won't stand much chance of winning the big race."

"You're right," sighed Patchy. "I'll have to stick a patch over this big hole in the hull, before it's even seaworthy."

"All the others, with their smart yachts, will laugh when they see ours," declared Miss T.

"Perhaps it won't look too bad when it's in the water," said Patchy. "I know, I'll blow a bit of fog round the worst bits, to hide them while we're getting the boat down to the sea."

Miss T. brightened up a bit as Patchy got his foghorn and started to blow puffs of fog round *Morning Cloud*.

Patchy only meant to let out a few puffs, but before he'd finished there was a great cloud of fog around the boat.

"Come on, let's get it moving towards the water," said Patchy. "We'll sing a shanty to help us keep in step, because that's what sailors do when they're working." He took a deep breath and began to chant:

"Always in a foggy flurry, I get nowhere in a hurry,
Though I really try to scurry - or Miss T. is sure to worry."

Miss T. could just hear his muffled voice through the fog and she replied:

"I'm Miss T., a little hazy, though I'm never ever lazy,
Patchy fog can send me crazy, making muddles that amaze me!

"Are we near the sea yet?" she called out.
"I don't know, I can't see a thing," puffed Patchy.
By this time the other Merryweathers were arriving on the scene.
"Whatever are they doing?" cried Ray the Sun.
"Tee hee, they're pushing the boat *away* from the sea," giggled Gus T.
"I'd better help them," decided Wayne Rain, running to the rescue.

At last they got thing sorted out and *Morning Cloud* was launched on the water. Then everyone else got their boats afloat, and the race began.

"This will be an easy race for us," chuckled Gus T. to Gale, who was sailing with him on their catamaran *Ocean Breeze*.

"All we have to do is blow hard into our own sail. One, two, three, *blow*!"

Gus T. and Gale both blew hard and their sail billowed out, and the waves rose higher. *Ocean Breeze* swept past the other boats, but the wind was so strong it made them all bump into each other.

"Hey, that's not fair!" they yelled.

HARRY
AVE

Most of the other boats soon got themselves sorted out and raced after Gus T. and Gale. But Wayne Rain had to stop and bale out all the water the big waves had splashed over the side of his umbrella boat, *The Briny Brolly*. "I'll have to do something to get up extra speed," he cried in dismay.

Then he had a bright idea. "I know, I'll put up my umbrella sail and use it like a propeller."

Then he started whirling it round, faster and faster, so that *The Briny Brolly* went skimming across the water as fast as a hovercraft.

But Wayne had forgotten that twirling his umbrella made the rain come down. The faster he twirled it, the heavier the rain became. Soon everyone was sailing through a heavy downpour.

"Oooh!" complained Crash Thunder. "This rain's beating into my face."

"It's splashing against my sunglasses, too," grumbled Ray, lifting them to see just how far behind Wayne was leaving him.

As soon as the rainstorm had passed, Crash began to move ahead in his metal boat, *Rumble Fish*. "At last I can get up some real speed," he chuckled, letting out his sail.

He was nearly overtaking Flash Lightning's yacht, *Sea Current*, when Flash looked down from his perch on top of the mast.

"Thunder can't go before me," he cried. "I'll soon put a stop to that."

Stretching out his finger, he sent streaks of lightning flashing towards the metal boat.

"Yow!" yelled Crash as he was shaken rigid by an enormous electric shock.

"Ho, ho," laughed Flash."That'll teach you not to overtake me!" But he didn't notice Harry Hail sailing along behind him in his little boat, *Stingray*.

Flash was still chuckling over the way he'd tricked Crash when Harry Hail saw his chance to get rid of them both. Whipping out his hailshooter, he aimed hailstones at Flash, who was an easy target as he sat on top of the mast.

Ping, ping, ping, Flash Lightning felt the shower of hailstones stinging him. "Ouch!" he squealed, toppling from his perch. Desperately he grabbed at a sail to stop his fall. But that made his yacht keel over and he landed on the deck of Crash's boat, with the sail on top of them both.

"Hee, hee, that's got rid of them," chuckled Harry, watching them fighting as he sailed past at great speed.

But faster still was Nippy Frost, who slid by on his gleaming white craft, *Icy Floe*.

Nippy was well in the lead. "I'm going to be first," he laughed. But then he looked behind him and saw the other boats were beginning to catch up.

"I'll soon stop them," he said and craftily pointed his finger at the water. The waves he chose turned to ice and suddenly the others saw a row of icebergs rising up in front of them.

"Look out! There's danger ahead," warned April, who was sailing along in her little canoe, *Raindrop*.

"Och, we'll never be able to cross that barrier," called Scotch Mist, in a rage.

"You're right, Jock," gasped Harry Hail. "He's really beaten us this time."

But Ray the Sun had seen Nippy's crafty cheating. "Two can play at *that* game," he said, rising from his boat and shining down on Nippy's ice boat.

Nippy found that *Icy Floe* was melting away, under his feet. "Help, my boat's disappearing," he cried in alarm. "I shall sink in a minute!"

All the others laughed and said it served him right for cheating.

"Now everybody must play fair from now on," declared Ray, reading out the Boat Race Rules.

By this time Nippy had been able to

freeze *Icy Floe* back into shape and the boats started off again.

But way behind everyone else, Patchy Fog was sitting at the tiller of his old boat. "I'm afraid *Morning Cloud* hasn't any chance of winning," he told Miss T.

"The other boats are slowing down," Miss T. pointed out. "Whatever is happening now?"

The Merryweathers had been making so much noise as they sailed towards the finishing line, that a whole school of dolphins had come close to see what all the excitement was about. Now they were leaping out of the water, right in the path of the leading boats.

"Look out," shouted Wayne. "We'll all have to sail round them," and he started off paddling in a different direction, with the others following.

"A boat race, what fun!" whooped the dolphins. "But perhaps we'd better clear the way or they won't get through."

GUS
HARRY

"This is going to be an exciting finish," declared the dolphins, as they all gathered by the finishing line.

But before the other boats could get back on the right course, shabby old *Morning Cloud* came sailing along and passed the finishing line first.

"Well done!" beamed Silvia Moon, who was waiting to present them with the winner's big silver cup.

None of the other Merryweathers were too disappointed, either, because Silvia had a small silver cup for each one of them who had *almost* won the boat race.